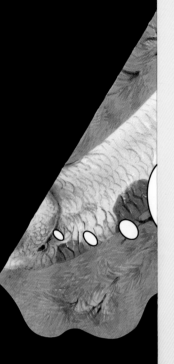

DINOSAURS

Illustrated by Peter Scott

Written by Alastair Smith and Judy Tatchell

Designed by Ruth Russell

Digital imaging by Keith Furnival

SCHOLASTIC INC.

New York Toronto London Auckland
Sydney Mexico City New Delhi Hong Kong

Gentle giants

Here are some of the biggest dinosaurs. They were much taller than giraffes, and much heavier than elephants.

Even the babies were as big as cows.

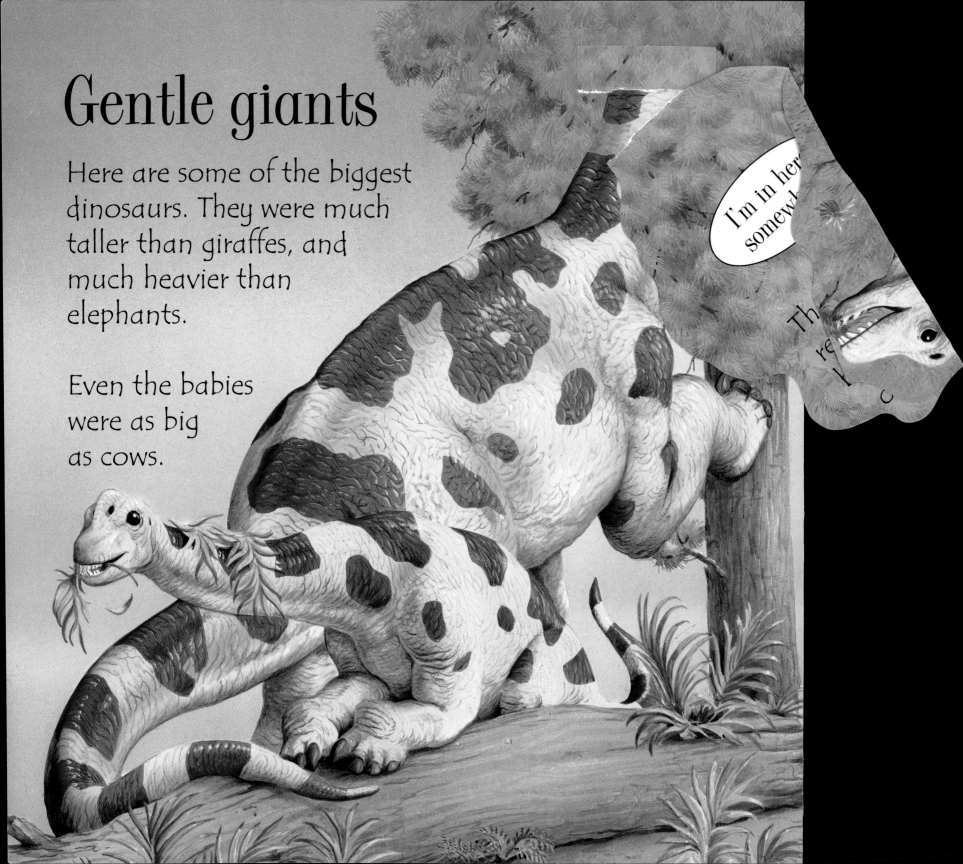

I'm in here somewh

These dinosaurs breathed through holes on top of their heads. Can you see the holes?

These dinosaurs are called brachiosaurs.

They didn't chew their food. They just grabbed it and swallowed it whole.

What's this dinosaur doing? Lift the flap to see.

Mothers and babies

Dinosaurs laid eggs, just like birds do. Babies hatched out of the eggs.

This dinosaur is putting leaves over her eggs to keep them warm.

This dinosaur is called a maiasaura.

If dinosaur eggs got cold, the babies inside would die.

Here are some more dinosaur eggs. A baby is coming out of one of them.

This kind of dinosaur is called an orodromeus.

Fast and fierce

This dinosaur hunted other animals.
It was big, strong, fast and fierce.
It's called a Tyrannosaurus rex,
or T-rex for short.

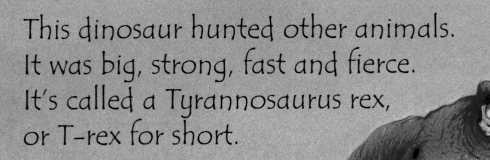

Its mouth was
full of sharp
teeth. It could
kill with just
one bite.

Two things on
a T-rex weren't
so big...

T-rex attacked with a
rush and a grab. It was
all over in seconds.

A T-rex's skin was tough and scaly. It was a little like a crocodile's skin.

Each T-rex was as long as a bus and as tall as a house.

A T-rex could smell animals even if it couldn't see them. Can you find an animal in danger?

I smell dinner!

In the air

These flying animals lived at the same time as the dinosaurs.

They weren't dinosaurs or birds though. They were called pterosaurs.

Whose tail is this?

Look at these huge wings. They were covered in leathery skin.

Each wing was as long as two grown-up people.

Can you see this pterosaur's arm, and its fingers?

This one could swallow fish whole. Look in its beak.

I'm a dinosaur. I'm small but I'm fierce.

In the sea

In the time of the dinosaurs, lots of fish and other creatures lived in the sea.

This is an ichthyosaur. It looked like a fish, but it breathed air, like you do.

When it was underwater, it held its breath. It could hold its breath for much longer than you can.

Ichthyosaurs were a little like dolphins, which live in the sea today.

Animals had to be careful in the sea. There were lots of scary monsters in the water...

Funny heads

Some dinosaurs had very funny-looking heads.

This one could make loud noises. Long tubes inside its pointy head made a trumpet sound.

They lived together, like a herd of cows.

Toot! Where are you?

This dinosaur is called a parasaurolophus.

This one had a big head shaped like a funny hat.

It had rows and rows of teeth in its mouth, to cut up tough, chewy plants.

It also had a big, heavy tail...

My friends think my head looks great!

This is a corythosaurus.

The front feet were like a duck's feet, with skin between the toes.

Rough stuff

These dinosaurs could look after themselves. They were very good fighters.

This one had a hard head. Perfect for head-butting.

This one had spikes on its head. Just right for jabbing.

This is a triceratops.

This dinosaur is called a pachycephalosaurus.

Today there are no dinosaurs.
They all died a very long time ago.

Additional design by Christopher Morris and Verinder Bhachu

ISBN 978-0-545-27420-3

12 11 10 9 8 7 6 5 4 3 2 1   10 11 12 13 14 15/0

Printed in Malaysia   108

This edition first printing, September 2010